T0029487

# The
# WISDOM of
# FLOWERS

# About the Author

**Liz Marvin** is a writer and editor. She has written *How to Be More Tree*, *The Secret Lives of Animals*, *Dog Speak* and *The Windowsill Gardener* for Michael O'Mara Books. She is a wildflower enthusiast and lives by the sea on the south coast of England.

# About the Illustrator

**Rosie Dore** is an illustrator and surface pattern designer based in Kent (UK), where she keeps bees and attempts to manage her ever-growing house plant collection. Guided by her love of wildlife and nature, she seeks to capture moments of connectivity to the natural world through detailed, textural and colourful illustration. To view more of her work, you can visit her website at www.rosiedore.com

# The
# WISDOM *of*
# FLOWERS

## Essential Life Lessons
## for Joy and Wellbeing

Liz Marvin
Illustrated by Rosie Dore

First published in Great Britain in 2023 by LOM ART, an imprint of
Michael O'Mara Books Limited
9 Lion Yard
Tremadoc Road
London SW4 7NQ

A CIP catalogue record for this book is available from the British Library.

This product is made of material from well-managed, FSC®-certified
forests and other controlled sources. The manufacturing processes
conform to the environmental regulations of the country of origin.

ISBN: 978-1-912785-89-6 in hardback print format
ISBN: 978-1-912785-98-8 in ebook format

1 2 3 4 5 6 7 8 9 10

www.mombooks.com

Designed and typeset by Ana Bjezancevic and Barbara Ward

Printed and bound in China

# Introduction

You have probably admired flowers for
their vibrant colours, eye-catching beauty
or elegant form, but have you ever stopped to
consider what lessons they may have for us?

Flowers are very wise. There is a lot we can learn from
the ways in which they grow, adapt and flourish. They
remind us to make the most of the sunshine but also
not to fear the grey days, as rain is also nourishing. They
affirm the value of community. They tell us when it is
spring, showing that better times always come around
again. And though they can be small and delicate, they
are often tougher and more tenacious than you might
think, surviving and thriving in all sorts of unexpected
places. Some may bloom exuberantly throughout the
season, others only once a century, or their flowers
may last just one night. But whatever their style, when
it is time to burst into bloom they never hold back.

In these pages, you will find sixty of the most
fascinating and surprising flowers from around
the world and the lessons they would like to
pass on about life, love, adversity and hope.

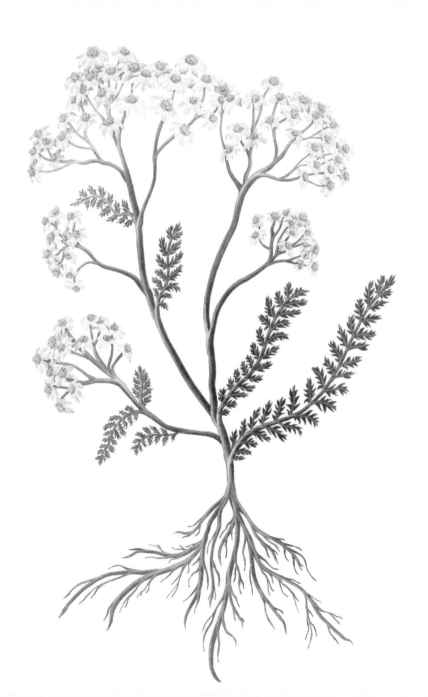

# Learn to heal

YARROW

*Achillea millefolium*

Yarrow is a tough little plant with a compassionate disposition. Its resolute nature means it tolerates different conditions – it will grow on the roadside as well as in flowerbeds. Since ancient times, it's been an important medicinal herb, used particularly to stanch the blood from wounds. In Latin, it is named for Achilles, the Greek warrior whose body was invulnerable to injury, except for his heel. So valued has yarrow been through the ages that it has a rich heritage in magic and folklore. It is said to mean both 'healing' and 'love', perhaps because you can't have the former without the latter.

# It's cool to
# be weird

## BAT FLOWER
*Tacca chantrieri*

Pretty pastels and vibrant shades are all too common
in the plant world. The bat flower, however, just
doesn't relate – and it refuses to conform. With its
black or purplish 'wings' and long whiskers, it has a
style all of its own. This is one flower that just loves
to be different and has made absolutely sure no one
is going to be confusing it with a geranium any time
soon. The bat flower says: let your freak flag fly.

# Respect your chronotype

## MOONFLOWER
### Ipomoea alba

In the plant kingdom, it's kind of the done thing to
make sure your blooms are open in the day. Most flowers
are early risers, ready to greet the dawn and all the
buzzy pollinators who are just waking up. Not so the
moonflower. It keeps its ghostly blooms tucked away in
the daytime, opening up after sundown and releasing
a delicate scent to attract the attention of moths and
other night-time travellers. So don't worry if you're not
a lark – listen to the wisdom of the moonflower and
embrace the peace and solitude of the dark hours.

# Turn your face to the sun

## SUNFLOWER
*Helianthus annuus*

There's a lot we can learn from these bold and cheerful flowers. In the growing phase, their circadian rhythm helps to turn their heads, tracking the sun's path across the summer sky. After sunset, they turn to face east again, excited to start a new day. When the sun shines on you, take a lesson from the sunflower and make the most of every minute. Seize the day – and if other tasks and chores can wait, let them. It's no wonder that in Chinese culture, sunflowers are said to mean good luck and lasting happiness.

# Make a home

## BUDDLEIA
### *Buddleja davidii*

The buddleia bush is a lot like the resourceful sort of person who can turn even the most run-down rented house into a beautiful and welcoming space. It is often spotted growing in the most unloved places, among derelict buildings and on waste ground. In late spring, it throws forth pretty purple or sometimes white blooms, attracting all the local butterflies for a joyous pollen party. The buddleia teaches us that, with a bit of enthusiasm and tenacity, almost anywhere can be made a bit more lovely.

# Rise above

## SACRED LOTUS
### *Nelumbo nucifera*

This ancient flower is full of meaning for people all over Asia. According to Buddhism, when Gautama Buddha took his first steps, lotus flowers appeared everywhere he stepped. The beautiful bloom is nourished by the mud at the bottom of the river – which, for Buddhists, represents our messy human lives – but it floats free, up on the water's surface, a powerful symbol of enlightenment. As a Zen verse has it: 'May we exist in muddy water with purity, like a lotus.'

# Never give up hope

## OLEANDER
### *Nerium indicum*

For the ancient Greeks, the elegant oleander flower
stood for charm and desire. For the people of Hiroshima,
it means something very different. After the atomic
bomb was dropped on the city, it was said nothing
would grow there for seventy years. Yet the following
year, oleanders bloomed, providing strength and
reassurance to a city trying to recover from devastation
and terrible trauma. The oleander shows us that
even after catastrophe, hope will always return.

# Don't fear the dark side

## COMMON SNAPDRAGON
*Antirrhinum majus*

In the spring and summer, these pretty cone-shaped flowers can be seen in gardens from Istanbul to Indiana. It's hard to believe that these easy-going and cheery blooms have a darker side, but they do. Come autumn, the flowers turn into eerie-looking seedpods and by Halloween look like tiny dragons, or even human skulls. Don't be too creeped out though, they are not a harbinger of doom – the oil from the seeds was believed to ward off witchcraft and sorcery.

# It's okay to lie low sometimes

## LITHOPS
### *Lithops weberi*

There's no getting away from it, this native of southern Africa is a funny little plant. It spends much of its life incognito, disguised as a pebble so as not to attract the attention of animals and to protect itself from the sun's glare. In drought conditions, it can even shrink below the level of the soil. But at a time that feels right – and only then – the lithops throws forth exuberant and unexpectedly large daisy-like flowers. The lithops says: take some time out if you need to; you'll know when you're ready to bloom again.

# You can't
# please everyone

## TITAN ARUM
*Amorphophallus titanum*

Also charmingly known as the 'corpse flower' because it
gives off an aroma a bit like rotting flesh, the titan arum
is hardly everyone's cup of tea. And yet this monstrous
flower is truly awesome – in the original sense of the word.
While its unappealing scent may repel some, others flock
to see this 6-10-feet purple wonder on the rare occasions
it blooms. When you're the biggest flower in the world,
though, you don't really care what anyone else thinks.

# Do something unexpected

## BAMBOO
### *Bambusoideae*

This remarkable plant is one of nature's hardest workers
and a special gift to humans. It has long been a vital
building material in its Asian home countries and is
associated with uprightness, tenacity and modesty
in Chinese culture. What bamboo is not known for,
however, is its blooms. And yet, sometimes only once a
century, for some reason the bamboo decides it's time
and the whole forest is hung with thin, papery blossoms.

Just because you are known for one thing, doesn't
mean you can't try something different for a change.

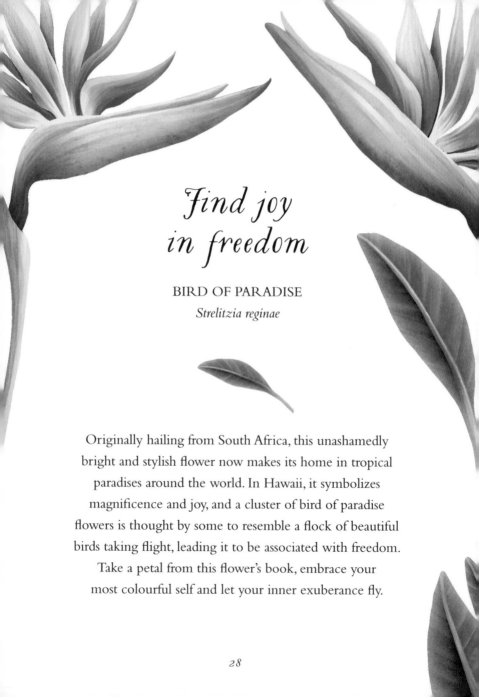

# *Find joy in freedom*

## BIRD OF PARADISE
*Strelitzia reginae*

Originally hailing from South Africa, this unashamedly
bright and stylish flower now makes its home in tropical
paradises around the world. In Hawaii, it symbolizes
magnificence and joy, and a cluster of bird of paradise
flowers is thought by some to resemble a flock of beautiful
birds taking flight, leading it to be associated with freedom.
Take a petal from this flower's book, embrace your
most colourful self and let your inner exuberance fly.

# Leave the world better than you found it

## CRIMSON CLOVER
*Trifolium incarnatum*

Clover flowers don't have to be accompanied by four leaves to be lucky. They were once considered a charm against hexes and bad spells. And, if you're a bee, a butterfly, a rabbit, a deer or even a cow, you might consider them lunch. These special plants also make the soil in which they grow more stable by binding it together with their roots, and more fertile by working with bacteria to fix in nitrogen, a greenhouse gas taken from the air. If a small flower can do its bit looking after the environment, then surely we humans can, too?

# Find your silver lining

## PINK FLANNEL FLOWER
*Actinotus forsythii*

Bushfires are a fact of life in Australia; the ecosystem
is built around a fiery clean-out once in a while.
However, in recent years, these fires have been especially
devastating, laying waste huge swathes of beautiful
national park. Among the blackened stumps, however,
there has been one cheering sight. The seeds of the
pink flannel flower can lie dormant for years until,
following a fire, they take the opportunity to grow
through the charred ground, decorating the landscape
with a carpet of tiny blush-coloured blooms.

# *Look forward*

WILD DAFFODIL

*Narcissus pseudonarcissus*

The cheerful yellow daffodil shares its Latin name with a very vain young man in Greek mythology who couldn't stop staring at his own reflection. This is unfair because, far from being self-regarding, the altruistic daffodil takes its responsibility as the herald of the start of spring in the temperate northern hemisphere very seriously. When the days are still grey and gloomy, and even when there is snow on the ground, the daffodil brings a ray of sunshine to remind us that better times are just around the corner.

# Rock what you've got

## FRENCH HYDRANGEA
### *Hydrangea macrophylla*

These beautiful and showy globe-like flowers are the jewel of any garden. They come in an amazing variety of colours and shades which, unusually, are determined by the soil in which they grow. Hydrangeas growing in more acidic soils are blue, whereas those in alkaline soils are a blushing pink. Their common name is a bit misleading, though, as they are actually native to Japan, where legend has it that an emperor gave a bouquet of blue hydrangeas to the woman he loved as an apology for neglecting her in favour of his business.

# Throw out the rule book

## NOBLE DENDROBIUM
### *Dendrobium nobile*

Plants need soil to grow, right? 'Not so!' says the noble dendrobium, a species of orchid that uses its roots to hang onto a tree or rock (known as epiphytes or lithophytes). They cleverly get all the water and nutrients they need from debris that falls into the cracks and crevices that they grow from. Orchids are said to represent love, beauty and strength. Be more orchid and do things your own way.

# Looks can be deceptive

## LILY OF THE VALLEY
*Convallaria majalis*

This beautiful plant has delicate white, bell-shaped flowers that hang down like old-fashioned babies' bonnets. Its delicate scent perfumes woodlands all over the northern hemisphere in late spring – it is the birth flower of those born in May and a popular wedding flower. In Christian legend, Mary's tears turned to lily of the valley as she wept by the cross. But be warned that this flower is not as defenceless as it seems; all parts of the plant contain toxins that can be harmful to dogs, cats and people if eaten. And it looks a little like wild garlic, which it sometimes grows alongside.

# *Don't let your environment define you*

## HYACINTH

*Scilla madeirensis*

Many plants would look at a rocky coastal clifftop with
dismay – what could possibly thrive up there, constantly
buffeted by salty breezes? This defiant hyacinth is not
to be deterred. Despite its relative lack of resources, it
makes the best of the situation and sends up a 2-feet-
tall stalk topped with an exotic lavender-blue cone of
flowers. Each autumn, they enjoy the magnificent sea
view, swaying gracefully in the warm Atlantic winds.
Different colours have different meanings in the language
of flowers – blue means constancy, appropriately
enough for these flowers that return year after year.

# *Thrive wherever you land*

## MOUNTAIN LARKSPUR
### *Delphinium glaucum*

Adaptable delphiniums make their homes everywhere
from African hills to English cottage gardens. Mountain
larkspur doesn't mind that it lacks the showy elegance
of its more cultivated cousins – this pioneering plant
has a rugged beauty all of its own, toughing it out in
mountainous terrain from Alaska to Arizona. Mountain
larkspur blooms are blue and in the language of flowers
this stands for dignity and grace, as well as constancy.
If you are born in July, larkspur is your flower.

# Embrace
## the mystical

### GIANT WATERLILY
*Victoria amazonica*

There is something distinctly otherworldly about the
giant waterlily flower. The white buds unfurl at night,
like an elegant ballerina dancing on a huge floating leaf.
Beetles are attracted by the heat the flower produces but
then the petals close around them, temporarily taking
them prisoner. The next day, the beetle is released, a
little dazed, to pollinate other waterlilies, and the flower
turns pink. According to legend, a girl fell in love with
the moon but was drowned when she tried to embrace
its reflection in the water. A sympathetic goddess
turned her into a beautiful flower – the waterlily.

# Take a chance

## IMPATIENS
### *Impatiens wallerina*

These cute little bedding plants — also known as Busy
Lizzies — are popular with gardeners for their colourful
blooms and laidback attitude. They don't mind a shady
spot and will grow happily in flowerbeds, pots and hanging
baskets. Their flowers turn into tight little seed pods that
burst open exuberantly with the tiniest touch, spreading
seeds up to 3 feet away. Sure, some seeds will land in rocky
places and never grow, but who knows what opportunities
might await the rest? The impatiens says: just go for it!

# *Let down your defences*

## COMMON GORSE

*Ulex europaeus*

The gorse bush is not a plant to be messed with, as it is notoriously spiky to deter passing herbivores who might fancy a nibble. Despite this, it provides a snug home for all sorts of bird and insect life. Its yellow flowers brighten up many a wild and windswept landscape. In some places, gorse flowers grow almost all the year round – hence the old Scottish saying, 'When the gorse is oot o'bloom, kissin's out of fashion.'

# Grow your
# own way

## STURT'S DESERT PEA
### *Swainsona formosa*

Some of us have so much in common with our family
that we are like peas in a pod, while others find it hard to
believe they share DNA with their nearest and dearest. The
second scenario is very much the situation for Sturt's desert
pea. These striking blood-red flowers can be found in
arid land all around southern and western Australia. Their
shiny black centres, known as bosses, make them look a
little like startled eyes. But although they are technically a
pea, they don't look anything like their legume relations.

# Bee whatever you want to bee

## BEE ORCHID
### *Ophrys apifera*

Imagine you're a flower but what you really want to be
is an insect. Well, the bee orchid – as its name suggests
– doesn't let simple facts of botany get in its way. It
embraces what its heart truly desires, putting on a stripy
outfit and living its truth. Boy bees land on it thinking
it's a lady bee, carrying away its pollen to the next flower.
Be more bee orchid and dress the way you feel inside.

# The value of stability

## BEACH MORNING GLORY

*Ipomoea pes-caprae*

As we deal with the shifting sands and ebbing tides of life, sometimes we just need to hold on tight. Beach morning glory understands this better than most. It is at home in salty coastal environments and its seeds can even survive an ocean dip. But it understands the value of staying rooted to one place, too. Its beautiful violet or white flowers can be seen tumbling down sand dunes from America to the Maldives, while its strong roots burrow into the sand, stabilizing the dunes by binding the sand so that other plants can move in.

# *Love conquers all*

## DOG ROSE
### *Rosa canina*

In Greek mythology, Aphrodite, the goddess of love, is
said to have cut her foot on a thorn as she rushed to
join her beloved Adonis as he died. Her blood stained
the white roses she passed, creating the red rose. Humans
have been passionate about roses for thousands of years,
breeding varieties that are ever more intricate. The wild
dog rose, however, is much loved for its simple, five-
petalled charm. The Rose of Hildesheim that grows over
a cathedral in Germany is said to be a thousand years
old and even survived an Allied bombing in 1945.

# Timing is everything

## NGUTUKĀKĀ

*Clianthus puniceus*

This unique and rare New Zealand native features
beautiful red flowers that hang in clusters, named after the
beak of the kaka parrot as they are the same sort of shape.
The shrub can grow up to 9 feet tall – but only when it
is ready. Its seeds can last for up to thirty years, waiting for
a landslip or tree fall to provide the perfect opportunity
to finally germinate. Patience is a virtue, but you've still
got to be ready to seize the day, says the ngutukākā.

# Go all out

## JADE VINE
### *Strongylodon macrobotrys*

There are very few jade vines left in the wild in their home in rainforests of the Philippines, but if you ever get to see one you are unlikely to forget it. These incredible flowers hang from stems up to 3 feet long. They range in colour from brilliant turquoise to pale mint green and appear luminous at twilight, like Chinese lanterns hanging from the rainforest canopy. This attracts tropical bats who, awed by their beauty, carry pollen from one to another. The jade vine says: put on your finery and dazzle.

# Don't take yourself too seriously

### BAT-FACE CUPHEA
*Cuphea llavea*

This is a flower with a quirky sense of humour.
Whereas not everyone would relish the epithet 'bat
face', this eccentric plant, originally hailing from
Mexico, loves its look and doesn't care what anyone
else thinks. It has bright red petals and a deep purple
centre that does look just like the face of a very small
bat. It's popular with butterflies and hummingbirds,
who love it for its bright colours and sense of fun.

# Only seek to control the controllable

## ENGELMANN PRICKLY PEAR
*Opuntia engelmannii*

Scorching days with the sun pounding down on your paddles. Chilly winter nights. Almost nothing to drink. Sandy soil and passing hungry wildlife. The Engelmann prickly pear knows the Sonoran Desert in south-west USA and Mexico isn't everyone's idea of comfort but hey, it's home. And this resourceful cactus has developed lots of clever ways to cope with what it can't change. Each of its yellow flowers only lasts for a day, but that's long enough to attract a passing pollinator. Make like a prickly pear and find your own unique way to deal with challenging situations.

# Wander far

ROSE-OF-SHARON

*Hibiscus syriacus*

No one really knows where the hibiscus comes from, but its passport is certainly well stamped. Its ancestors hailed from Mauritius, Fiji, Madagascar, Hawaii, China and India. Over the years, it has roamed tropical equatorial regions and been adopted by gardeners all over the world. *Hibiscus syriacus* is known as rose-of-Sharon in North America, after a story in the Bible. It is the national flower of South Korea, where it is called the *mugunghwa*, and is even celebrated in a line in the country's national anthem.

# Build a community

## WILD MARJORAM
*Origanum vulgare*

These small, modest flowers may lack the elegance of
a tropical orchid or the cheery exuberance of a bank
of daffodils, but they are very important to all who
live near them. From June to September they provide
welcome pollen to lots of different insects, including
butterflies, bees, beetles and hoverflies. They also aren't
fussy about where they grow: scrubland, grassland,
roadside – it's all the same to these generous and
outgoing little plants. Which just goes to show that you
don't have to be a big deal to make a big difference.

# Cultivate strength

## PLUM BLOSSOM
### *Prunus mume*

The cherry blossom may get all the press, with festivals
dedicated to it — called *hanami* — all over Japan, but the
plum blossom is loved throughout East Asia, too. The
white or pink flowers may look delicate, yet they bloom at
the very end of winter and, even when there is still snow
on the ground, their delicate perfume floats on the cold
air. For this reason, plum blossom symbolizes resilience,
perseverance and hope. And perhaps shows that you
don't need to look tough to be tough when necessary.

# See where the tide takes you

## SEA POISON TREE
*Barringtonia asiatica*

The flowers of the sea poison tree look like a cross between a fluffy pompom and a sea anemone. Quite appropriate really, as its seeds are very buoyant and can be carried for hundreds of miles in the ocean currents until the tide washes them ashore. There, they wait for a bit of rain to rinse the salt off and they're good to go. Fish beware, though. As its name suggests, the fruits contain poison, which was traditionally used to stun fish for easy capture.

# Learn from adversity

## PASSION FLOWER
### *Passiflora*

The heliconius butterfly sees the passion flower as
perfect food for its caterpillars. However, the passion
flower disagrees and has come up with some innovative
solutions to deter the butterfly from laying eggs on its
leaves. It can change the shape of its leaves, sometimes
fooling the butterfly with this clever disguise. The leaves
are also mildly poisonous and have little bumps that look
like eggs to make the butterfly think that leaf is already
taken. The passion flower knows that difficult challenges
can present opportunities to come up with new ideas.

# Be generous

## COMMON LILAC
### Syringa vulgaris

Catching the beautiful scent of the lilac flower on a
warm evening is a sure sign that summer has arrived.
So intoxicating is its perfume that the ancient Celts
concluded that the lilac tree must be in possession of
magical powers. In Russian folklore, holding lilac over
a newborn was thought to bestow the gift of wisdom.
If lilac blooms are brought into the house, however, the
scent can become cloying and overpowering, so leave
them on the tree where they can be enjoyed by all.

# Do it your way

## STARFISH FLOWER
### *Stapelia grandiflora*

Dr Seuss wrote, 'Why fit in when you were born to stand out?' The starfish flower would definitely agree, as it's a plant that very much dances to its own tune. These strange-looking flowers grow on the ground, looking much more like something you'd find on the seabed rather than in a flowerbed. Unusually in the flower world they are often dark purple or brown and they smell a little like, well, rotting meat, hence their other name, 'carrion flower'. The starfish flower says: 'Whatever works for you!'

# Get your gang together

## YELLOW FLAG IRIS
*Iris pseudacorus*

Irises are rhizomatous plants, meaning that they spread by
pushing out root-light stems horizontally just below the
soil's surface. Each rhizome has little nodules from which
new shoots can grow. So what looks like several individual
plants can actually be a whole gang sharing a common
rhizome. The yellow flag iris is one such plant. Growing
around ponds and streams, these guys are passionate about
caring for their environment and work together to filter
out toxins, purifying the water for all who live nearby.

# Be proud of what you can do

## LAVENDER
*Lavandula angustifolia*

Lavender is at least 2,500 years old, giving it plenty of
time to have developed an array of impressive talents.
In traditional medicine it's used as a treatment for
insomnia and modern studies have confirmed that it is
beneficial for helping you get to sleep. Its flowers are
popular with bees, who use the nectar to make delicious
honey, while bugs that humans find pesky are repelled
by its strong scent. So take time to develop your own
skills, however humble or modest you might think
them, and bring joy to you and others around you.

# Cherish
# your rituals

## PŌHUTUKAWA
### *Metrosideros excelsa*

Much loved in New Zealand as a symbol of strength
and beauty, this tree bursts into glorious flower around
December, leading to one of its nicknames: New Zealand's
Christmas tree. It is a very important tree in Maori
culture as the red flaming flowers are said to represent
the blood of a warrior who fell to earth after attempting
to reach heaven to find help to avenge his father's death.
We all have different rituals and beliefs, so observe and
celebrate yours in whatever ways make sense to you.

# Stand your ground

### THISTLE
*Cirsium vulgare*

Once the thistle arrives, it is not leaving. Its main root,
or taproot, can be over 2 feet long, and its spikes mean
that most grazing animals steer well clear. Despite its
rather prickly nature, however, its purple flowers are
packed with nectar and loved by many insects. It is the
national flower of Scotland because, according to legend,
an invading Norseman once stood on a thistle in bare
feet, alerting the nearby clansmen to his whereabouts.

# Practise compassion

## FALSE BIRD OF PARADISE
*Heliconia rostrata*

This eye-catching plant is found in the rainforests of South and Central America. What look like vivid flowers growing up the stem are actually known as bracts. Hummingbirds and butterflies are drawn to the flowers' nectar, while tiny aquatic organisms live in the water that collects in the bracts. Mosquitoes also breed here, which may not sound that appealing, but the heliconia thinks that everyone deserves a chance – even the less popular members of the insect world – and is happy to provide accommodation.

# *Be bold*

## BUTTERCUP
### *Ranunculus repens*

According to folklore, if the light of a buttercup
held under your chin reflects on your skin then it
means you like butter. But scientists decided this
explanation of the buttercup's brilliant yellow colour
was somewhat . . . unscientific. They concluded that
the reason for the flower's iridescent shine is a layer of
air beneath the surface that reflects light like a mirror
to signal to passing pollinators. Some butterfly and
bird wings do this too, but the buttercup is unique in
the plant world in having this skill. The buttercup says:
shine bright and the bees won't be able to resist.

# *Innovate*

## BURDOCK
### *Arctium lappa*

The no-nonsense burdock flower is purple and spiky, but
what is really clever is what it does next. After flowering,
the seedhead develops with little hooks. This easily
separates from the plant and attaches to the fur of any
passing mammal. This way, the burdock's seeds can travel
far further than the plant could manage by itself. George
de Mestral invented Velcro after studying this phenomenon,
so inspired was he by the burdock's creativity.

# *Break the rules*

## BOUGAINVILLEA
### *Bougainvillea glabra*

The first Europeans to catalogue this beautiful plant
were part of an expedition led by Admiral Louis
Antoine de Bougainville, after whom it is named. But
it seems that the sample was collected and logged by
Jeanne Baret, a pioneering female botanist posing as
a man at a time when women were not allowed on
French ships. The bougainvillea has a similar disregard
for convention. For example, what you might take
for flowers are actually brightly coloured specially
adapted leaves with tiny flowers nestling inside.

# Do more with less

## DESERT ROSE
*Adenium obesum*

Hailing from the Arabian peninsula where water supplies
are low at best, the desert rose has developed a tactic to
make the most of what it has. Unusually for a succulent
it has a 'trunk' which it uses to store water. This gives it
a stout look rather like a pot-bellied Buddha, which has
endeared it to people in South-East Asia, who associate it
with longevity and wealth. The desert rose is not wealthy,
of course – merely saving up for a non-rainy day.

# *Upskill*

### TREE RHODODENDRON
*Rhododendron arboreum*

The beloved national flower of Nepal – where it is
known as *Lali gurans* – this rhododendron has a number
of talents. The flowers are pickled, dried for tea and used
for medicine, and beautiful bowls are made from the
fine-grained wood. The blooms (which change colour at
different altitudes) are a much-welcomed sign of spring.
Though recently, not content to rest on its laurels (another
plant entirely), this rhododendron has been flowering even
earlier, to try to warn humans about climate change.

# Take care

### FLAME LILY
*Gloriosa superba*

Also known as a glory lily or a tiger's claw, these statuesque
blooms can be found in many different habitats across
Africa and South Asia. Although they have been used in
traditional medicine for centuries, this is a flower not to
be messed with – it is poisonous and has even been used
to commit murder! The flame lily says: there is no need
to go through life feeling afraid, but it's wise to be alert
to danger and know when you are playing with fire.

# *Seasons change*

## SEA ASTER
*Aster tripolium*

These beautiful purple wildflowers are also known as
Michaelmas daisies, as in Northern Europe they bloom
around the feast of St Michael, on 29 September, which
is near the autumn equinox and traditionally the time
of year by which the harvest should be gathered in.
Known in the English counties of Dorset and Somerset
as 'summer's farewell', these asters remind us that
there is a season for everything and you often have
to say goodbye to the old to welcome in the new.

# Life is full of surprises

## WILD VIOLET
*Viola sororia*

These beautifully scented little purple flowers bloom
enthusiastically in the spring in Europe and Asia. Their
superpower is that they self-seed widely and can pop up
in all sorts of unexpected locations, where the previous
spring there were no flowers at all. Shakespeare loved
violets and mentions them often in his plays. They may
be the wanderers of the flower world but, surprisingly,
they are still believed to symbolize faithfulness.

# *Paint the town red*

## LIPSTICK TREE
*Bixa orellana*

This tree believes the world needs to be more colourful
and is happy to help out. Its pretty pink blooms
turn into furry pods, which split to reveal clusters of
seeds containing bixin, a vivid red pigment that has
been used in body paint for thousands of years and is
still used in cosmetics today. Whether you are more
inclined to a sultry red lip or all-over body paint,
embrace colour and don't be afraid to be seen.

# Don't let others tell you who you are

## WALLFLOWER
### *Erysimum cheiri*

Originally hailing from Greece, these exuberant flowers
have a strong scent and come in many different colours.
They are as popular with butterflies and other pollinators
as they are with gardeners, who have made them welcome
in flowerbeds around the world. You can imagine the
wallflower's surprise, then, to learn that the expression
'to be a wallflower' means to be shy and retiring! But the
wallflower just shrugged and remembered another saying
– what other people think of you is none of your business.

# Treat yourself!

## CHOCOLATE COSMOS
### *Cosmos atrosanguineus*

This native of Mexico eschews the heady scent of lilacs or the pretty perfume of violets for something closer to its heart – its deep reddish-brown flowers smell uncannily like chocolate and vanilla. After all, this plant grows in the land of the Mayans, who revered chocolate and drank it with almost every meal. The cosmos believes that pleasures are there to be enjoyed and we should embrace life's small joys.

# Be a pioneer

## DANDELION
*Taraxacum officinale*

Whenever land has been cleared dandelions are the
first in, dispersing their seeds like a little advance
parachute regiment. Before long, their yellow heads
can be seen bobbing in the sunshine, their strong
taproot dug resolutely into the ground. It's this spirit
that makes them so successful – dandelions are found
on six continents and, as any gardener knows, they
are very hard to get rid of! It takes courage to be the
first, to break new ground, but it's better than always
hanging back and waiting for others to go ahead.

# Compassion means patience

## ARTICHOKE THISTLE
### *Cynara scolymus*

Humans have been eating artichoke as a delicious vegetable for so long that we might have forgotten that it is actually the bud of a fascinating flower. We can be forgiven for this, as artichokes contain a higher concentration of health-boosting antioxidants than most vegetables. But if they are allowed to bloom, the spiky and tough outer leaves unfurl to reveal spectacular 6-inch purple blooms. If you want to know what's hiding behind someone's tough exterior, you might need to give them time and space, and they will show their inner selves when they are ready.

# Romance never dies

## KISS-ME-OVER-THE-GARDEN-GATE
*Persicaria orientalis*

Flowers have always been associated with romance and love. Floriography means the language of flowers and Victorians would give each other bunches with meaning coded into the blooms. Kiss-me-over-the-garden-gate can grow to over 9 feet tall and gets its name from the flirty way its flowers droop down and 'kiss' you as you walk past. Along with other heritage cottage garden flowers that have been around for hundreds of years – such as love-in-a-mist, cupid's dart or forget-me-not – this pretty flower reminds us that flowers are fleeting but romance will always capture our hearts.

# Rainy days will come

## SKELETON FLOWER

*Diphylleia grayi*

Flowers and humans alike, we all love to bask in the sun.
Happy days of sunshine help us to grow and flourish
but it's important to remember that those grey, overcast
days when rain is bound to come can be nourishing
as well. When they get wet, the delicate white petals
of this amazing woodland flower become transparent,
exposing the veins to make it look like an exquisite glass
skeleton. The skeleton flower reminds us that beautiful
things can emerge even in less favourable conditions.

# Miracles can happen

## ST HELENA EBONY
*Trochetiopsis ebenus*

These elegant white flowers are native to St Helena, a remote volcanic island in the southern Atlantic Ocean. For over a hundred years, they were thought to be extinct, eaten by goats introduced to the island by passing explorers. Then a local guide spotted through binoculars the last two remaining plants tucked away on a cliff. He made the precarious climb and more ebony plants were grown from cuttings he carried back in his teeth. The story of the St Helena ebony shows that you should never give up hope – but you should always be wary of goats.

# Seize the day

## NIGHT-BLOOMING CEREUS
*Peniocereus greggii*

If you were walking past this cactus in its home in the
Sonoran Desert any day of the year you would take it for
a dead bush. But then, on just one night in June or July, it
bursts forth in a dazzling and ethereal display of fragrant
white blooms, which all wilt away by the next morning.
It's so rare to see that parties are thrown in its honour.
This remarkable flower that appears and is gone so soon
reminds us that there is so much magic and wonder in our
world – we just have to keep our eyes and our hearts open
so we can appreciate these moments when they occur.

# Index

| False bird of paradise *p.91* | Flame lily *p.103* | French hydrangea *p.36* | Giant waterlily *p.47* | Hyacinth *p.43* |

| Impatiens *p.48* | Jade vine *p.63* | Kiss-me-over-the-garden-gate *p.119* | Lavender *p.84* | Lily of the valley *p.40* |

| Lipstick tree *p.108* | Lithops *p.23* | Moonflower *p.11* | Mountain larkspur *p.44* | Ngutukākā *p.60* |

| Night-blooming cereus *p.124* | Noble dendrobium *p.39* | Oleander *p.19* | Passion flower *p.76* | Pink flannel flower *p.32* |

Plum blossom
*p. 72*

Pōhutukawa
*p. 87*

Rose-of-
Sharon *p. 68*

Sacred lotus
*p. 16*

St Helena
ebony *p. 123*

Sea aster
*p. 104*

Sea poison
tree *p. 75*

Skeleton
flower *p. 120*

Starfish flower
*p. 80*

Sturt's desert
pea *p. 52*

Sunflower
*p. 12*

Thistle
*p. 88*

Titan arum
*p. 24*

Tree rhododendron
*p. 100*

Wallflower
*p. 111*

Wild daffodil
*p. 34*

Wild
marjoram *p. 71*

Wild violet
*p. 107*

Yarrow
*p. 7*

Yellow flag iris
*p. 83*